SUPER SMART
INFORMATION
STRATEGIES

USING DIGITAL MAPS

by Adrienne Matteson

CHERRY LAKE PUBLISHING • ANN ARBOR, MICHIGAN

CHERRY
LAKE
Publishing

A NOTE TO PARENTS AND TEACHERS: Please remind your children how to stay safe online before they do the activities in this book.

A NOTE TO KIDS: Always remember your safety comes first!

Published in the United States of America
by Cherry Lake Publishing
Ann Arbor, Michigan
www.cherrylakepublishing.com

Content Adviser: Gail Dickinson, PhD, Associate Professor, Old Dominion University, Norfolk, Virginia

Photo Credits: Cover, ©Roberto Caucino/Shutterstock, Inc.; page 4, ©Joe Ravi/Shutterstock, Inc.; page 5, ©Andresr/Shutterstock, Inc.; page 6, ©Carolina K. Smith MD/Shutterstock, Inc.; page 9, ©Iain Masterton/Alamy; pages 10, 11, 12, 13, 15, 20, 21, and 27, ©2012 Nokia ©2013 Microsoft Corporation; page 14 and 28, Imagery ©2013 Commonwealth of Virginia, DigitalGlobe, District of Columbia (DC GIS), Sanborn, U.S. Geological Survey, USDA Farm Service Agency, Map data ©2013 Google, Sanborn; page 18, ©Vasily Kovalev/Shutterstock, Inc.; page 19, ©Vasily Kovalev/Shutterstock, Inc.; page 24, ©Lissandra Melo/Shutterstock.com; page 25, ©Nadasazh/Shutterstock, Inc.; page 26, Imagery ©2013 TerraMetrics, Map data ©2013 Google.

Library of Congress Cataloging-in-Publication Data
Matteson, Adrienne, author.
  Using digital maps / by Adrienne Matteson.
      pages cm. — (Information explorer)
  Summary: "Explore the world by learning how to use digital maps." — Provided by publisher.
  Audience: Grades 4 to 6.
  Includes bibliographical references and index.
    ISBN 978-1-62431-129-1 (lib. bdg.) — ISBN 978-1-62431-261-8 (pbk.) — ISBN 978-1-62431-195-6 (e-book)
  1. Digital maps—Juvenile literature. 2. Digital mapping—Juvenile literature.
  I. Title. II. Series: Information explorer.

  GA139.M37 2014   2013012084
  910.285—dc23

Cherry Lake Publishing would like to acknowledge the work of The Partnership for 21st Century Skills. Please visit www.p21.org for more information.

Printed in the United States of America
Corporate Graphics Inc.
July 2013
CLFA13

Table of Contents

CHAPTER ONE
Discovering Digital Maps

There are many different things to see in Washington, D.C.

Your family has decided to visit Washington, D.C., this summer! You'll be driving there, and your parents are letting you help plan the trip. You know Washington, D.C., is the capital of the United States, but you have a lot of questions about the city. Where is it? How long will it take to get there? Are there any interesting places to stop along the way? What is there to do once you get there? You will need to do a little research to answer these questions. Where do you start?

A digital map is a good place to begin. Digital maps can be accessed using the Internet. They can show you everything from the street layout of a small town to an overview of the entire world. A digital map also allows you to look at many different kinds of information about the area you are interested in. Most digital maps can be set to show **political features** such as roads, highways, and city names. You can also use them to look at **physical features** such as rivers, lakes, and mountains. Depending on which digital map **application** you choose, you may also be able to save your own notes and pins to the map.

Digital maps can help you and your family plan a road trip.

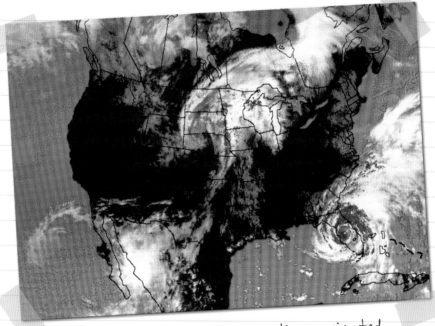

Satellite images are sometimes animated on digital weather maps.

There are different digital maps for different purposes. Weather Web sites, such as Weather.com and WeatherBug, use digital maps to show satellite images of moving storms or temperature changes. MapQuest is a digital map Web site designed specifically for travelers. It gives driving directions and helps users find hotels, restaurants, and shops. Google Earth is actually a digital globe! It reflects the way the earth curves, and it shows buildings, mountains, and even the ocean floor in 3D. These map sites are useful in different situations. You will need to determine which one best suits your needs. You might even need to use more than one at a time.

TRY THIS!

Compare and contrast three popular digital map applications: Google Maps (http://maps.google.com), Bing Maps (www.bing.com/maps), and MapQuest (www.mapquest.com).

Search for your hometown on each Web site. Then ask yourself questions: How easy is this map site to use? What kind of information does it show? What does it have that the other map sites do not? Make a chart to help you organize your thoughts!

To get a copy of this activity, visit www.cherrylakepublishing.com/activities.

DID YOU KNOW THIS?

When you use an Internet search engine such as Google or Bing, you might get a few results that are marked as sponsored links. The same is true when you look up a place using a digital map application.

These links are not normal search results. They are paid advertisements. These sponsored results are highlighted in a different color near the top of the list. They are usually not as helpful as the regular search results beneath them. Be sure to keep alert and have a clear idea of what kind of results you are looking for.

Google

ADVERTISING

CHAPTER TWO
Finding a Location

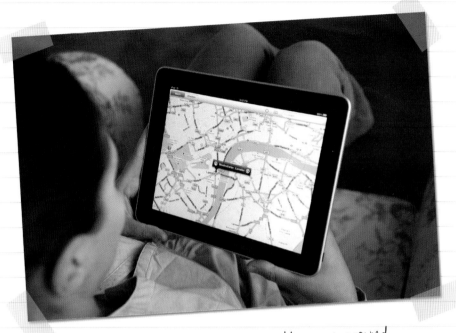

Most map sites let you move the map around to see surrounding locations.

You've chosen the digital map that's a good fit for planning your Washington, D.C., trip. What should you do next? The best way to begin any digital map search is to locate the place you want to go. Locating the city will help you see where it is and give you a good idea of how to get there.

As in any Internet search, you can search for terms that are very general or very specific. If you want a map of the entire city, simply type the city's name into the search box at the top of the screen. When you type

"Washington, D.C." and click Search, a list of results will appear next to the map screen. One or more colored flags, or pins, will appear on the map. One of them will mark the place you are searching for. Now you can see where Washington, D.C., is!

If you need to find a specific place in the city, such as a museum you plan to visit or the hotel where your family is staying, search for the exact address. When you search for an address, include as much information as you can. The more detailed the address you type in, the more likely you are to find the result you are looking for. Type the address into the search box. Begin with the name of the building. Use commas to

An address search can include a place's street number, street, town, state, zip code, and country.

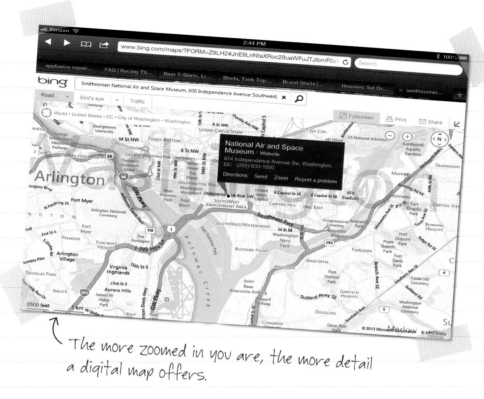

The more zoomed in you are, the more detail a digital map offers.

separate the different parts of the address. For example, you might type "Smithsonian National Air and Space Museum, 600 Independence Avenue Southwest, Washington, D.C., 20560."

When you search for a specific address, the map will most likely zoom in closer than it did when you searched for the city as a whole. This ability to zoom in and out is part of what makes digital maps so useful. On most maps, the symbols that indicate the zooming tool are plus and minus signs. As you zoom out, you will see a larger area of land. Only major locations will be labeled. When you zoom in, you will see more detailed labeling, but the map will cover a smaller area. If you zoom in all the way, you'll be able to see individual street names and even specific buildings!

You've located Washington, D.C. You zoomed out to see the surrounding areas and zoomed in to see streets and buildings. Now what? It's time to look around! Your digital map has a lot of tricks up its sleeve. It will take some exploring to discover them.

Most digital maps can change to provide different information. This is called changing the view. The main view is what most applications call the map view (Bing Maps calls it the road view). This view shows roads, highways, and state and country borders. The map view will also show rivers and lakes. This view is useful for finding your way and getting directions.

Map view sometimes includes labels for parks, important buildings, and major landmarks.

Satellite view is made up of photos taken from above.

But what if you don't want to see the roads and labels? You want to see what Washington, D.C., really looks like from the sky. That calls for a change of view. Most digital maps have a view called satellite. Bing Maps calls it the bird's-eye view. This is a great way to think of it. The satellite view allows you to see the land the way the birds do—without lines and labels. When you select satellite view, you can see physical features such as mountains, hills, and trees. You will also see actual roads, the roofs of buildings, and even swimming pools!

While this is called the satellite view, not all of the images used to make it are taken from satellites. Most of the images that make up the satellite view are taken from helicopters and airplanes. This view looks like one continuous picture of the earth. But it is really millions

of smaller photos put together! If you explore the satellite view closely enough, you may even come across places where no picture is available. This is because there are not as many photographs of places where only a few people live.

If you choose, you can see both map view and satellite view together. Google Maps calls this the hybrid view. This means it is made of two different things put together. In other maps you might be given the option to show labels while you are looking at the satellite view. This is great for when you are looking at a very zoomed in map. It lets you see what the place really looks like, but still gives you important information such as street names.

What if the satellite view isn't detailed enough for you? You want to see what it really looks like on the ground in Washington, D.C. A digital map can do that! Maps connected to larger Internet search engines, like Bing and Google Maps, have a lot of information to draw from. Look for an icon on the map screen that is shaped like a little person. Drag and drop the little person onto a street in Washington, D.C. The view will change to a ground level photograph of that street. The map will not have photos for every street. The streets that will work are highlighted when you click on the little person.

FYI

If you are using a digital map on a mobile device with a touch screen, such as a smartphone or a tablet, you might not see the bar or plus and minus signs for zooming. This is because maps made for touch screens let you zoom out by pinching two fingers together. You can zoom in by spreading your fingers apart. Try rotating, or turning, your fingers while they are touching the map. What happens?

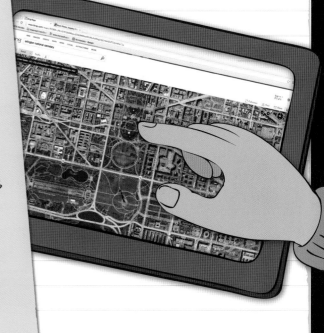

The street view is more than just a picture. You can change the direction you are facing and even click on other points in the photo to move down the street. It's like taking a walk inside the map!

While you are practicing switching views and zooming, look around the map screen for a circle with the letter *N* at the top. This is the compass. Like the compass rose on a printed map, this compass tells you which direction is north. By clicking on the sides of the compass, you can move around little by little on the map.

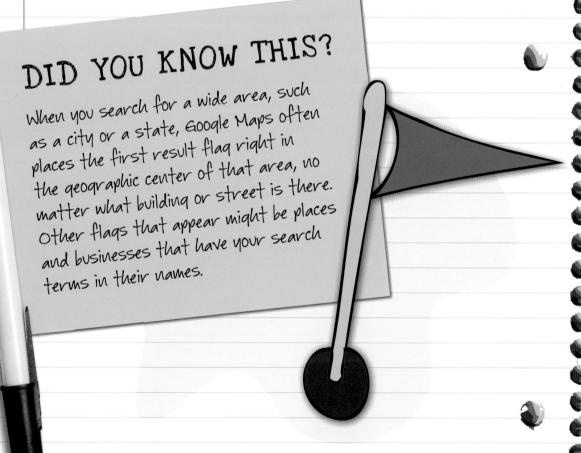

DID YOU KNOW THIS?

When you search for a wide area, such as a city or a state, Google Maps often places the first result flag right in the geographic center of that area, no matter what building or street is there. Other flags that appear might be places and businesses that have your search terms in their names.

TRY THIS!

Make a list of five or six places your family visits often. For example, you might list your school, your favorite stores, and your parents' places of work. First, try locating each of these places by searching using the name only. Don't include the city or state in your search terms.

Take notes for each location. How many results did you get? What kind of results did you get? Was this an effective way to locate this place?

Next, try locating each place with its exact address. (You might need your parents' help finding the correct addresses.) Ask yourself the same questions. Which search was the most effective? Can you think of situations when each kind of search would be the best?

To get a copy of this activity, visit www.cherrylakepublishing.com/activities.

CHAPTER THREE
Getting Directions

↳ A scenic route to a location may be prettier but is often longer.

The next step is planning your **route** to Washington, D.C.! A route is the path you plan to take to get from one place to another. You choose a route when you walk from one classroom in your school to another, or from your house to a friend's house. Sometimes you choose the route that is the fastest or the shortest. You might choose a route because of a stop you'd like to make along the way, or even a place you would like to avoid on the way.

As you and your family plan your drive to Washington, D.C., you have a lot of decisions to make. First, you need to decide what is most important to you. Do you want the drive to be fast? Beautiful? Interesting? The fastest route might not be the most beautiful, and a drive that includes the most interesting stops probably won't be very fast.

Your family decides to plan a route that will include a few interesting stops, including the Antietam National Battlefield for your dad, who likes to learn about the history of the Civil War. Because a route has a beginning and an end, the Get Direction search option in a

Antietam National Battlefield includes the battlefield site, a visitor center, a field hospital museum, and more.

digital map application always has two search boxes. Usually these boxes are labeled "A" and "B," but they might be labeled "Begin" and "End," or "From" and "To." Regardless of what the search boxes are called, the first box will always be your starting point. The second box is your **destination**.

When searching for directions, it is important that you put in the complete addresses for both places. This time the application is going to tell you *exactly* where to go every step of the way, so you should be as accurate as possible.

Now, the fun begins! Under the search boxes will be a lot of information for you to sort through. One of the first things you will see is an **estimate** of how

Map sites provide a distance and time estimate for each route.

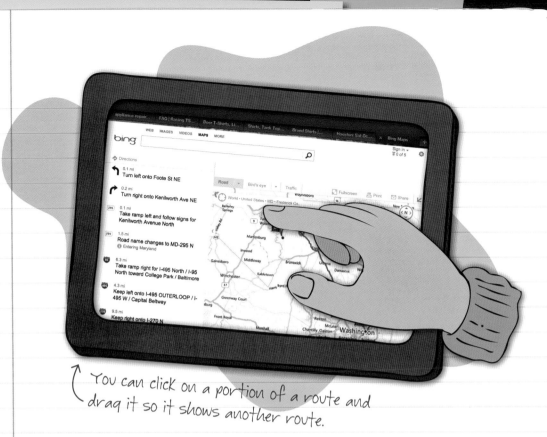

You can click on a portion of a route and drag it so it shows another route.

much time it will take to reach your destination. The search will also display the distance you will travel, measured in miles. There will be a list of the driving directions written out, usually with small icons to show which direction to turn at each stop. There may also be suggestions for different routes to take. If you click on one of these alternate routes, you'll see the path highlighted on the map change. The list of directions below the search boxes will also change. This isn't the only way to make changes to the route, though. On most digital maps, you can click and drag the route line to make your own changes. If you want to be more exact, select the option to add a destination or stop. You can add as many stops as you want. The map will plot them for you.

DID YOU KNOW THIS?

Your map will automatically show you the best route for driving when you search for directions. But most digital maps can also show you the best route to take if you are using public transportation, walking, or biking! Did you know that it would take 235 hours to walk from Indianapolis, Indiana, to New York City?

Why make changes to the route? The map automatically creates a route that is the fastest trip between two places. But is the fastest route the best choice for you? Consider the drive to Washington, D.C. The purpose of the drive from your home to Washington, D.C., is not just to get there quickly. This drive is also to see new and interesting things on the way. The drive is a part of your family vacation, and you want to get the most out of it! After getting the recommended route on your digital map, you remember that your dad wants to visit Antietam National Battlefield. The battlefield is near Sharpsburg, Maryland, just off the highway on your route to Washington, D.C. When you adjust your route to include Sharpsburg, it changes the list of driving directions. It also adds about 25 minutes to the estimated driving time. Now that you have your route, it's time to plan what you will do when you get to Washington, D.C.

TRY THIS!

Search for the route from your home to your school. If you don't know your school's address, ask a parent or teacher. Next, use a digital map to plot a route that stops at four of your favorite places on the way to school.

Add each stop one at a time. You can either click and drag the route on the map or use additional search boxes. Can you do it without making the route cross or backtrack on itself? How many additional minutes will it take you to get to school with the added stops? Try different routes to see if you can make the drive shorter!

To get a copy of this activity, visit www.cherrylakepublishing.com/activities.

CHAPTER FOUR
Dropping Pins

Include any places you want to visit, such as the Smithsonian National Museum of Natural History, in your travel plans.

To start making plans for your time in Washington, D.C., you will need to gather a lot of information:

- Which places do you want to visit? Are some more important to you than others?
- Which places are close to each other? Can you visit them on the same day?
- When do the museums you want to visit open? Do you need tickets for a tour?
- Will you need to drive to some of those places, or can you walk to everything you want to see?

Wouldn't it be easiest to keep all of this information in one place? Of course it would! You can mark the places you want to see and write down other important information on a map. If you were using a printed map, you could do this with pens, highlighters, and sticky notes. It might get a little messy, but it would be easy to save. Saving your notes to a digital map is easy, too.

Saving maps requires creating an online account with the map service you are using (Google for Google Maps or Microsoft for Bing). If you are under 13 years old, you will need your parents' help with this. Ask them if they will create a Google or Microsoft account that you can use, or if they will allow you to save maps to an account they already have.

You may need to ask for help setting up an online account.

Once you are logged in, you will see a My Maps or My Places tab. When you click on My Maps, you will be given the option to create a map. You can give your map a name and a description. Now you are ready to begin editing it.

Some new tools will appear on the map screen. These can be used to add pins to mark the places you want to visit. You can change the colors and shapes of the pins to show what kind of places they are marking or how important the places are to you. You might give each person in your family a different color pin. That way you can make sure you are not visiting places that only one person wants to see. Each pin you place on the map has its own information box. This box is where you can save notes of your own. Take some time to explore the other editing tools. You never know what will come in handy.

Your saved maps will be available under a separate tab or button.

SAFETY FIRST!

Do you want your saved map to be public, so anyone using the Internet can view it? Make sure you take the steps necessary to keep your maps private. Look for the map settings and uncheck the box labeled "Public" or "Share." Be alert! Anytime you save personal information to a Web site, you need to double-check that it will stay private.

TRY THIS!

If you choose, you can share a saved map with friends who also have access to an online account. Try creating a map of the top five places you hope to visit someday. Choose a pin color and add a note to each place explaining why you want to go there. Then share the map with your friends. Ask them to add pins and notes of their own. When you are finished, you will have a map you've created together with your friends!

The great thing about having a map saved to an online account is that you can access it from any device you use. So you can create your map on the desktop computer at home and then open it on a tablet or smartphone on the road!

To get a copy of this activity, visit www.cherrylakepublishing.com/activities.

CHAPTER FIVE
Tip of the Iceberg

↖ Sites like Google Maps make tons of additional information available.

Consider for a moment what it means to use a map that is part of Google. It is connected not only to the Google search engine but also to the millions of people who use Google apps around the world. This means that the map you see is the tip of an information iceberg. What you see is just a tiny piece of the information you can find there. If you dig deeper, you will find you can choose to include many different elements in your map:

• Icons for Wikipedia links for places on the map

- YouTube videos recorded in different places on the map
- Pictures people all over the world have taken and shared using Panoramio, Google's photo sharing site
- Links to **webcams** and video that has been taken as recently as within the last hour

All of this might actually make Google Maps the wrong choice for you, depending on what you want to do with your map. It might be better to use a simpler tool, or one that was designed for exactly what you want to do. More isn't always better. But all of these choices show you just how connected everyone is. And these extra options can be a lot of fun if you spend time learning how to use them.

As you explore more with digital maps, think about how you might use different features in the map sometime in the future. What is useful to you, and what is not? Did you find anything surprising or interesting? Have fun! The great thing about an information iceberg is finding out how deep it goes.

TRY THIS!

Locate your hometown or another city you know well in Google Maps. Then check everything in the selection menu—traffic, Wikipedia, videos, pictures, bike paths, etc. You might need to expand the menu to find them all. Then explore!

To get a copy of this activity, visit www.cherrylakepublishing.com/activities.

Glossary

application (ap-luh-KAY-shuhn) a computer program that performs a certain task

destination (des-tuh-NAY-shuhn) the place a person is traveling to

estimate (ES-tuh-mit) a rough guess or calculation about an amount, distance, cost, or other quantity

physical features (FIZ-i-kuhl FEE-churz) the natural features of the land, such as rivers, lakes, and mountains

political features (puh-LIT-i-kuhl FEE-churz) features of the land created by people, such as roads, borders, and place-names

route (ROUT) the road or course that you follow to get from one place to another

webcams (WEB-camz) video cameras that broadcast directly to Web sites so that people online can watch

Find Out More

BOOKS

Boyer, Crispin. *National Geographic Kids Ultimate U.S. Road Trip Atlas*. Washington, DC: National Geographic, 2012.

Cunningham, Kevin. *Types of Maps*. New York: Children's Press, 2013.

WEB SITES

Google Maps Street View Gallery

http://maps.google.com/intl/en/help/maps/streetview/gallery/index.html

Check out some cool places to explore using Google Maps Street View.

National Geographic Kids: Quiz Your Noodle GeoBee Training

http://kids.nationalgeographic.com/kids/games/puzzlesquizzes/quizyournoodle-geography-bee

Test your map skills by taking this fun geography quiz.

Index

About the Author

Adrienne Matteson is a school librarian, and she thinks it's the best job in the world. She loves to travel, and she used to live and teach in South Korea. Now she lives in Indiana with her cat, George.